From a rock tomb at Deir el Gebrawi,
Egypt, c. 2400 B.C., Dynasty VI.

by Gordo

Or   in the U.S.S. *Constitution*, famous

AN EGYPTIAN REED SAILING BOAT ON THE NILE RIVER

A one-poled mast would have pulled a reed boat apart, so a bipod mast was used to spread the stresses.
The boat was steered by two long paddles. A huge Egyptian ship that sailed the east coast of Africa
and belonged to Queen Hatshepsut may be found in the *Bellerophon Coloring Book of Ancient Egypt*.

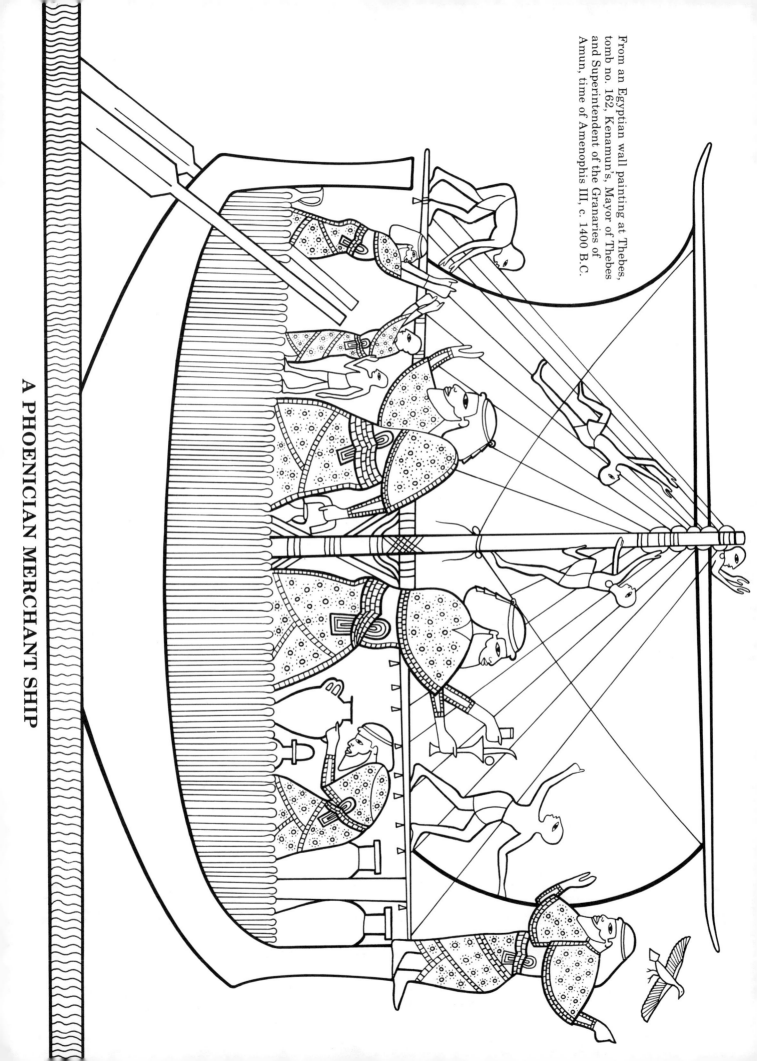

A PHOENICIAN MERCHANT SHIP

From an Egyptian wall painting at Thebes, tomb no. 162, Kenamun's, Mayor of Thebes and Superintendent of the Granaries of Amun, time of Amenophis III, c. 1400 B.C.

From a scene of Sennacherib's expedition to Phoenicia, from a relief from the
Palace of Sennacherib, now in the British Museum. Assyrian, c. 700 B.C.

A PHOENICIAN WARSHIP

The Phoenicians, who came from the eastern end of the Mediterranean, were
famous traders and great sailors. They may have developed
the two-banked galley, which made it possible
for a ship to be just as fast as a one-banked
boat but allowed it to be shorter and stronger.
A raised deck in the center, to the inner
side of the rowers, could be
used by passengers or
by fighters.

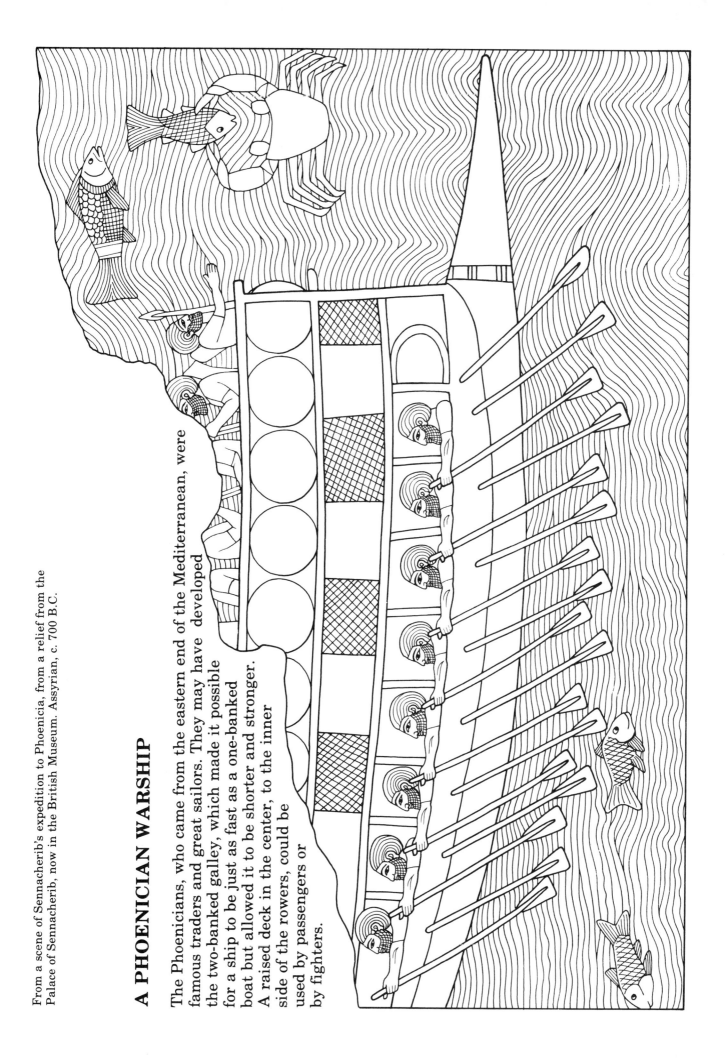

From a Greek black-figure cup by Exekias, 6th century B.C., Museum Antiker Kleinkunst, Munich.

AN ANCIENT GREEK SAILING SHIP

Dionysus, god of the vine, is sailing here in a ship whose ram is shaped like a boar's head and whose stern ends in a swan's head. Because he is a god, Dionysus is shown very large in relation to the ship. This picture illustrates the story of Dionysus and the pirates. Not knowing he was a god, they took him prisoner on their ship. But Dionysus then made grape and ivy leaves to grow around the ship and its mast. The pirates became so frightened that they jumped overboard and were turned into dolphins.

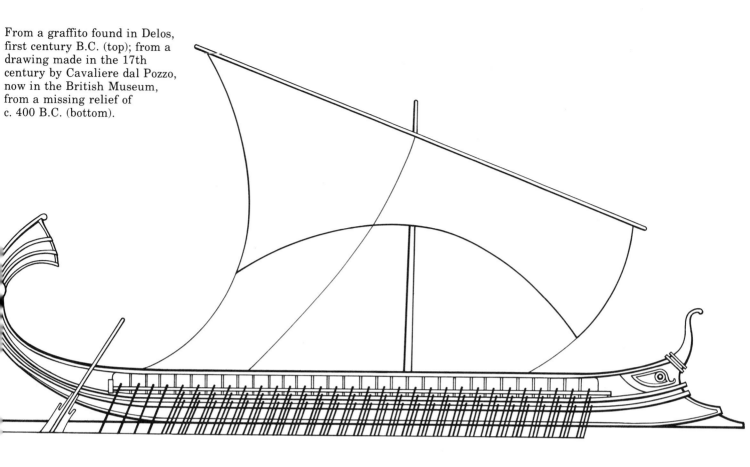

From a graffito found in Delos, first century B.C. (top); from a drawing made in the 17th century by Cavaliere dal Pozzo, now in the British Museum, from a missing relief of c. 400 B.C. (bottom).

GREEK TRIREMES

Triremes were oared war-ships propelled by three groups of rowers. The top group rested their oars on an outrigger which projected beyond the hull. The second line of rowers sat beneath them with their oars just below the gunwale of the ship. The bottom row sat within the ship just barely above the waterline. Triremes were light ships and did not usually travel far from land. In battle Greek commanders often used triremes to ram enemy vessels with their pointed prow.

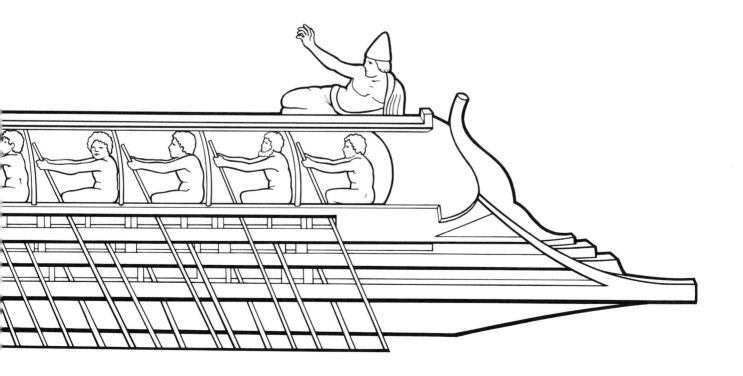

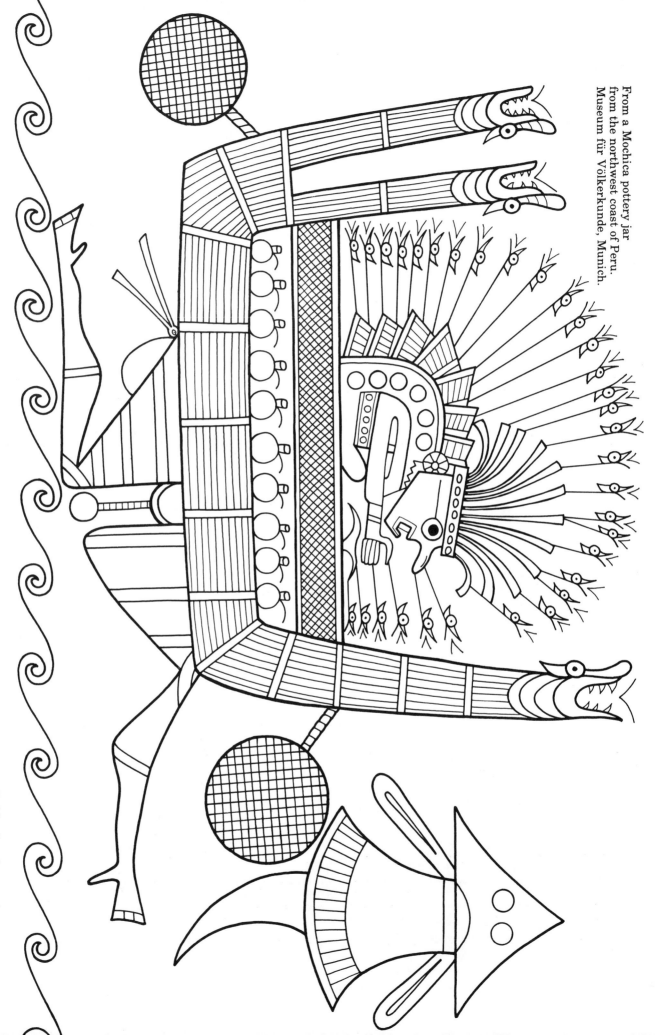

From a Mochica pottery jar from the northwest coast of Peru. Museum für Völkerkunde, Munich.

The reed boats of ancient Peru were similar to those of ancient Egypt. Timber was not available for dug-out canoes, but the reed craft could go several miles out to sea for fishing. Larger vessels were made with logs of light balsa wood tied together. These were driven by both sail and oars, and were large enough to hold 50 people. A ship of this kind was found by Pizarro's men in 1527, trading up and down the Pacific Coast.

From the François Vase by Kleitias,
570 B.C. Florence, Museo Archeologico.

HOW ANCIENT GALLEYS LANDED

The ships were backed up on the beach, stern first. This is probably why the last oar on the ship below is being taken off. The mast above has been lowered. One man has decided to swim ashore.

From a
black-figure hydria,
sixth century B.C., Louvre.

From a relief found at Ostia,
the Roman port at the mouth of the
Tiber River, now in the Torlonia
Museum, Rome. c. 200 A.D.

A ROMAN CARGO SHIP

This ship has *brails* for gathering up the sail, ropes which go through rings attached to the
sail. It also has a top sail, a new feature. The ship was probably a little more than 100 feet long.

from the *Pala d'Oro* in
aint Marks, Venice.
2th century.

AN EARLY SHIP FROM VENICE

The riches of the East reached Europe in Venetian ships, and Venice became the most important trading city in Europe because of her connection with Constantinople. Charlemagne tried to conquer Venice, and Arabs defeated Venetian sailors, but soon Venice was trading with them, too. The Crusades made Venice even richer, and the Fourth Crusade, led by Venice, conquered Constantinople.

From the Seal of Dover, 1284.

A SHIP OF THE 13TH CENTURY

The ships of the 11th and 12th century were not very different from the Viking long ships, but when sail power became more important than oars, ships were built larger in order to carry more sail. About the only pictures of northern ships of the 13th century are on the seals of sea-port towns, and these made the ships seem shorter than they really were. This ship was about 75 feet long and 25 feet wide. During the 13th century temporary towers, fore and after castles, were added for fighting, and a bow sprit came into use; this allowed longer lead for the bowline, which held taut the windward edge of the square sail, so the ship could sail closer into the wind. This seal belongs to one of the Cinque Ports, towns on the southeastern coast of England which thrived because of their nearness to the Continent, and from which the English kings borrowed their ships in time of war.

From an English bestiary from the end of the 12th century, Oxford, Bodleian Library, ms. Ashmole 1511.

AN ENGLISH SHIP   **OF THE 12TH CENTURY**

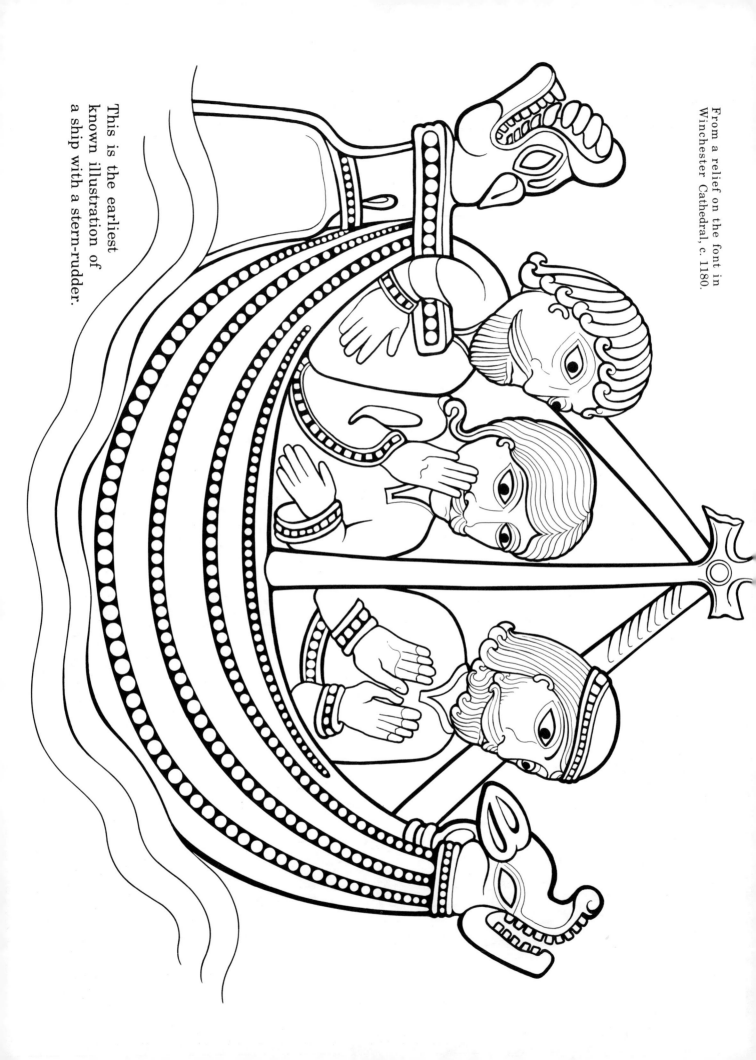

From a relief on the font in Winchester Cathedral, c. 1180.

This is the earliest known illustration of a ship with a stern-rudder.

The magnificent craftsmanship of the Viking ships was the result of centuries of Norse shipbuilding.

THE PROW OF THE OSEBERG SHIP

Several beautiful Viking ships have been found and restored; the most famous is the Oseberg ship, now in the Viking Ship Hall, Oslo.

This ship was discovered in 1903 buried near Oslo Fjord in Norway. It was built about 850 A.D. and was used as a burial-chamber for a great Viking lady. Like all early Northern ships she is clinker-built, which means that each strake, or plank, was riveted overlapping the strake below; on the Oseberg Ship the 12 strakes are attached to the ribs by lashings of whalebristle. Rich equipment was found on board including 15 pairs of oars, a beautiful cart, 3 beds, 3 sleighs and a sled, 2 tents, and a wagon, all covered with wonderful carvings. There were also 10 horses. The ship had been broken by time into thousands of small pieces, and restoration was an enormous task. The Oseberg ship, 70 feet long, was a small, light ship. Big Viking warships had 30 or more pairs of oars, and Canute's ship with 60 pairs of oars was 300 feet long!

A colorful helmet of a great Viking chief will be available shortly from Bellerophon Books, ready to cut out and put together.

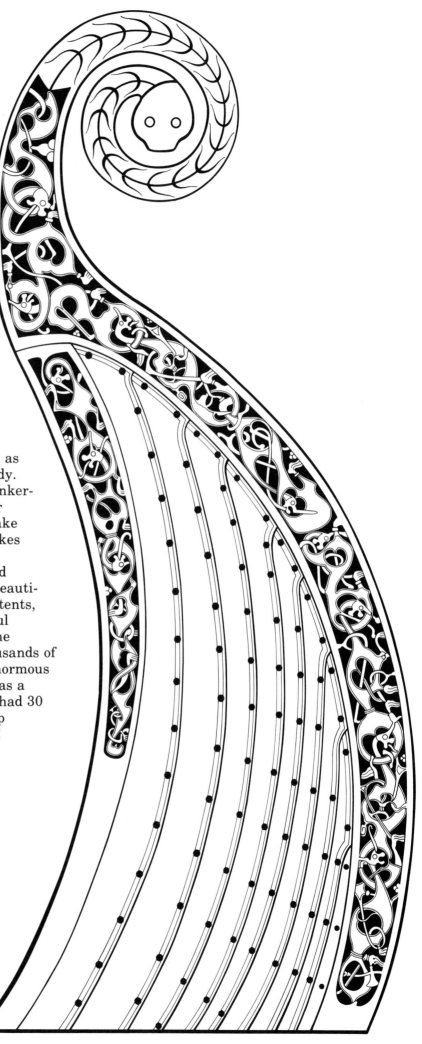

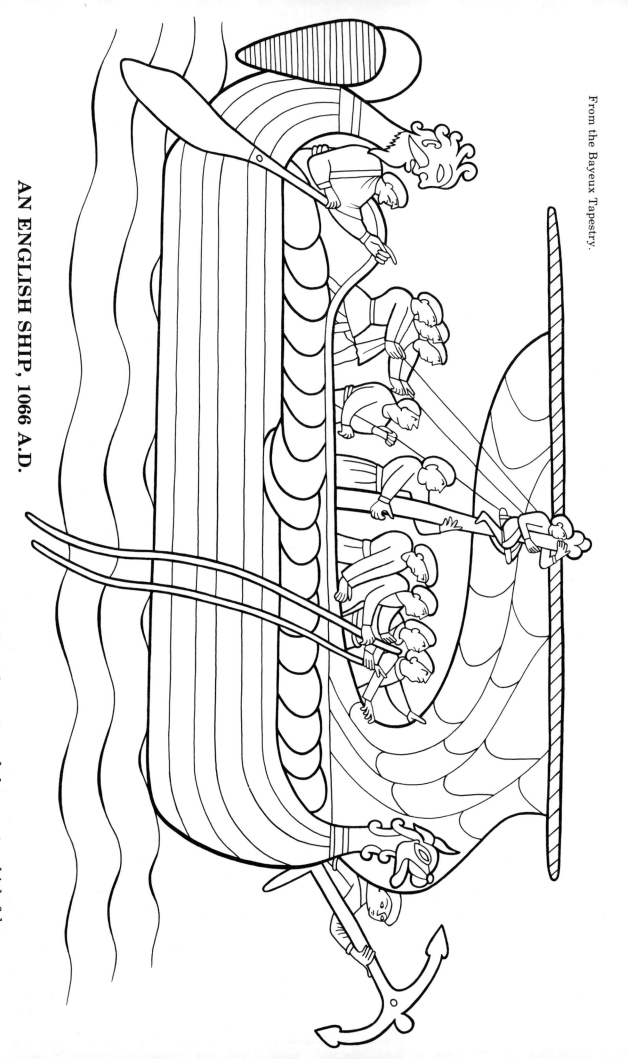

From the Bayeux Tapestry.

AN ENGLISH SHIP, 1066 A.D.

In this scene, King Harold's ship is about to drop anchor on the French coast, and the events which follow lead to the Norman conquest of England by William the Conqueror, descendant of a Viking chief.

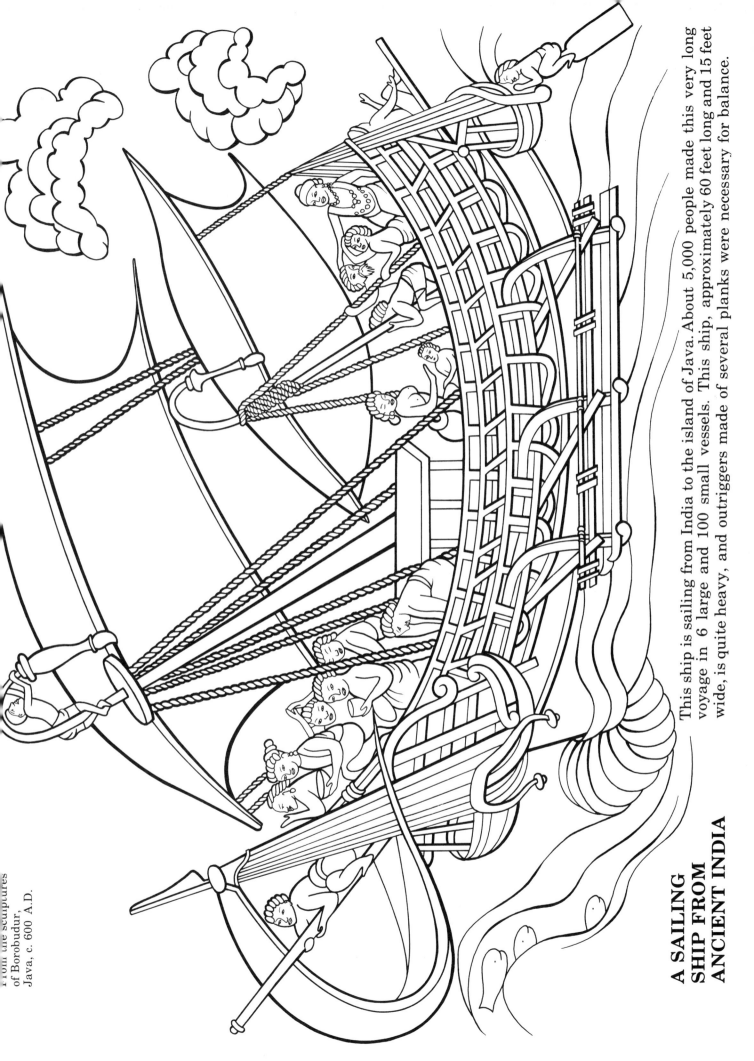

From the sculptures
of Borobudur,
Java, c. 600 A.D.

This ship is sailing from India to the island of Java. About 5,000 people made this very long voyage in 6 large and 100 small vessels. This ship, approximately 60 feet long and 15 feet wide, is quite heavy, and outriggers made of several planks were necessary for balance.

**A SAILING
SHIP FROM
ANCIENT INDIA**

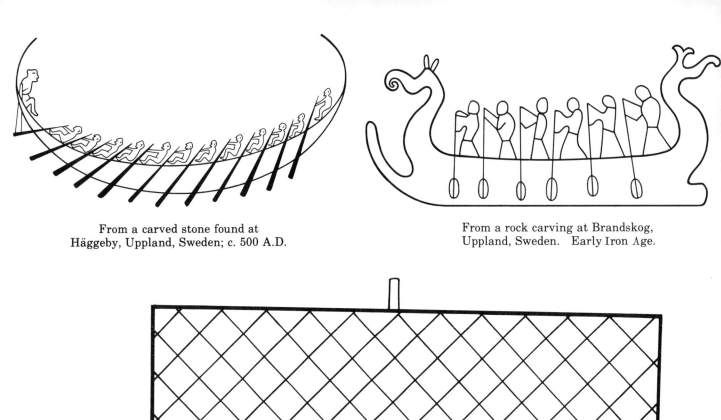

From a carved stone found at
Häggeby, Uppland, Sweden; c. 500 A.D.

From a rock carving at Brandskog,
Uppland, Sweden.   Early Iron Age.

**A
VIKING
SHIP**

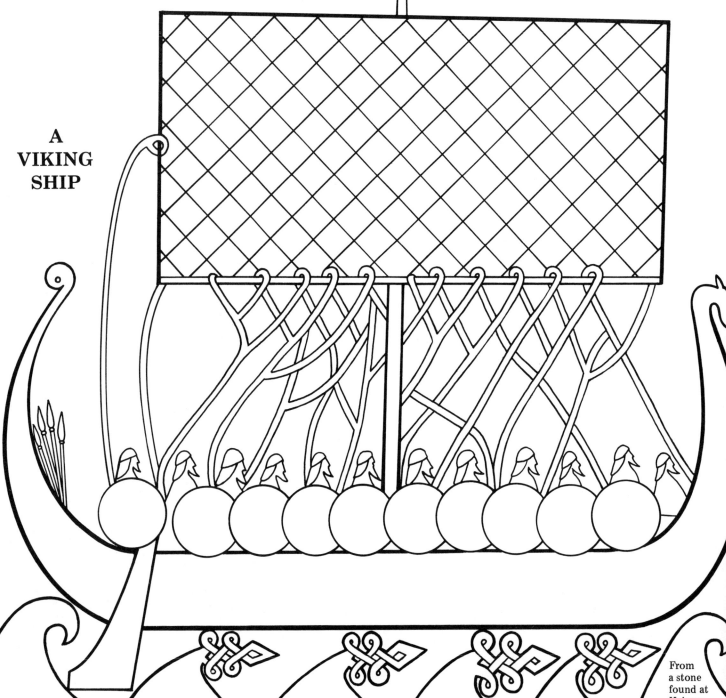

From
a stone
found at
Hejnum,
Gotland;
8th century.

AN ARAB SAILING SHIP

From a manuscript of el-Hariri's
Maqamat in the Bibliothèque Nationale,
Paris, ms. *arabe* 5847. 1237 A.D.

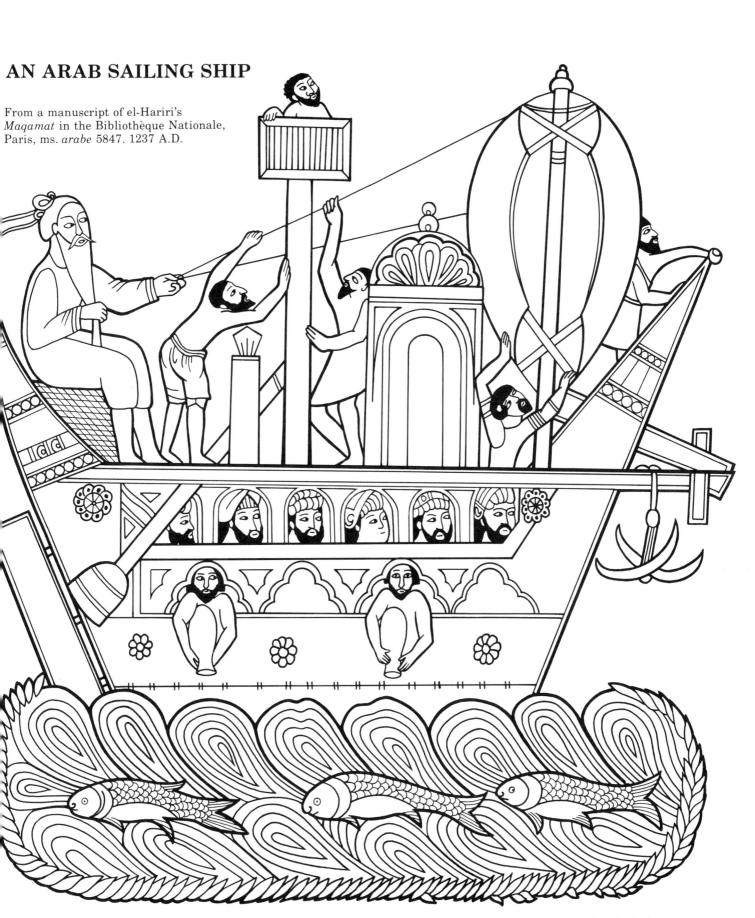

Mohammed died in 632, and within two years his followers were carrying the faith overland with great armies, and soon, overseas with great navies. In 648 an Arab Fleet of 1700 ships took Cyprus, and by 711 Arab ships crossed the Straits of Gibraltar, and all of Spain was captured. For several centuries Arab sailors controlled most of the Mediterranean Sea. They sailed in ships like this, but with more knowledge of sailing than had the artist who made this picture. Many great advances in navigation came to Europe by way of the Arabs, and our word *admiral* comes from the Arabic *el miro*, or chief.

From the third scroll of the Life of Gisho, 13th century; Kozan-ji, Kyoto.

From a relief on the shrine
of St. Peter Martyr, Church
of St. Eustorgio, Milan, by
the Pisan sculptor Giovanni
di Balduccio, 1339.

AN ITALIAN SAILING SHIP OF THE 14TH CENTURY

The detail on the relief from which this picture has been taken is much better than that found in illuminations or seals. We can see the large deck beams coming through the outer planking of the ship, and one of the two side rudders, with all the complicated and ingenious rudder-tackles.

From the seal of Thomas Beaufort, Earl of Dorset
and Duke of Exeter, Admiral of England, 1404.

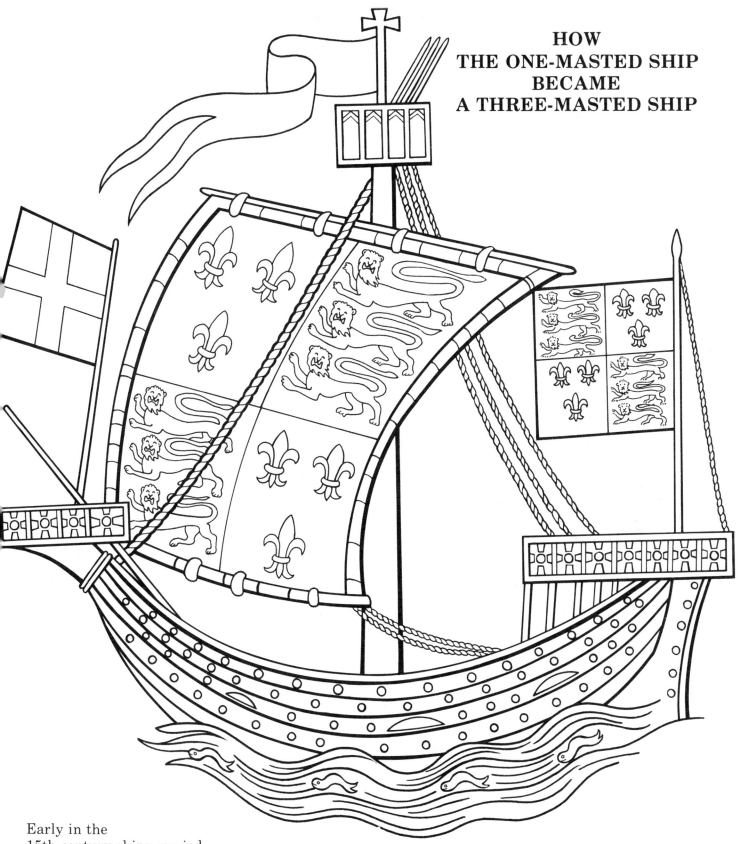

HOW
THE ONE-MASTED SHIP
BECAME
A THREE-MASTED SHIP

Early in the
15th century ships carried
three flag staffs: in the bow, in the stern, and
on top. By the middle of the century sails were
set on them, and athey became foremast, mizzen,
and top mast. A very huge ship from about this
period, Henry V's *Grace Dieu,* launched in 1418,
lies in mud flats in the Hamble River in England. This ship measures 135 feet by 37 feet,
and her mast is estimated to have weighed 29
tons. The ship probably required a crew of 200
mariners, since its gear was so heavy. This great
ship should surely be rescued soon and restored.

From an engraving by
the Master W. A., c. 1470.

AN EARLY THREE-MASTED SHIP

At the beginning of the 15th century sea-going sailing ships had only one
mast and one sail, but by the date of this picture the three-masted, full-rigged
ship had arrived. The sailing ship was to remain essentially the same for
the next four hundred years. This southern ship was probably Dutch owned.

From the manuscript *Pageant of Richard Beauchamp, Earl of Warwick*, 1389-1439, drawn 1485. British Museum, Cotton ms. Julius E. IV.

Howe Earle Richard in his commyng into Englond wanne ij greet Carykkes in the See.

The three-masted ship was introduced about 1460. Here we can see the use for which the projecting forecastle was built—to provide a good fighting position.

From a drawing by Jean Jouve, Marseille, 1679,
Bibliothèque nationale, Cabinet des Etampes, Paris.

A VENETIAN GALLEASS

The galleasses developed
from the *galia grosa,* the
heavy Mediterranean merchant
ship of the 15th century. It was a
greatly enlarged galley and carried
many more guns, especially on the
broadside where the galley had none.
It was driven by huge lateen sails
as well as by oars, and each
oar had five men behind it.

From an engraving after Stradanus, 16th century.

CHRISTOPHER COLUMBUS SHOOTING THE SUN

Columbus used a system developed by the Portugese for finding latitude by the noonday sun. But, he wrote to King Ferdinand and Queen Isabella, "neither reason nor mathematics nor maps were of any use" in his discoveries.

From Breydenbach's *Peregrinations*, 1488.

A SHIP SIMILAR TO
THE SANTA MARIA
SAILED BY COLUMBUS TO THE NEW WORLD

A woodcut probably copied from this was used in 1493 to illustrate the translation of Columbus' letter to Rafael Sanchez, the treasurer of the King of Spain, in which the great discoveries were announced. The *Santa Maria* has often been called a *caravel,* a Portugese type of lateener (with the kind of sail found on the galleass in the center of this book). The *Pinta* and the *Niña* were originally built as *caravels* (and later re-rigged as in the picture above), but the *Santa Maria* was always a square-rigged ship.

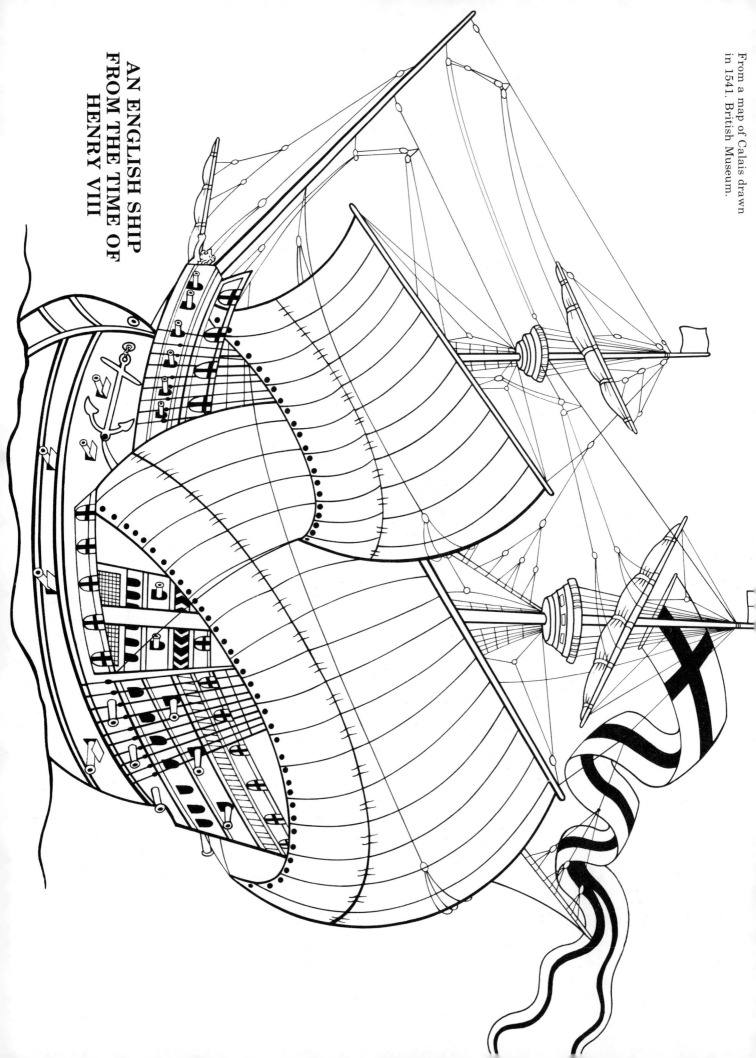

AN ENGLISH SHIP
FROM THE TIME OF
HENRY VIII

From a map of Calais drawn
in 1541. British Museum.

From a late 15th-century manuscript of Josephus. Österreichische National-bibliothek, Vienna. ms. 2538.

A
FOUR
MASTED
SHIP

The southern way
of caravel planking,
with the edge of one
plank against the edge
of the next, now began to
replace the old northern
method of overlapping planks.

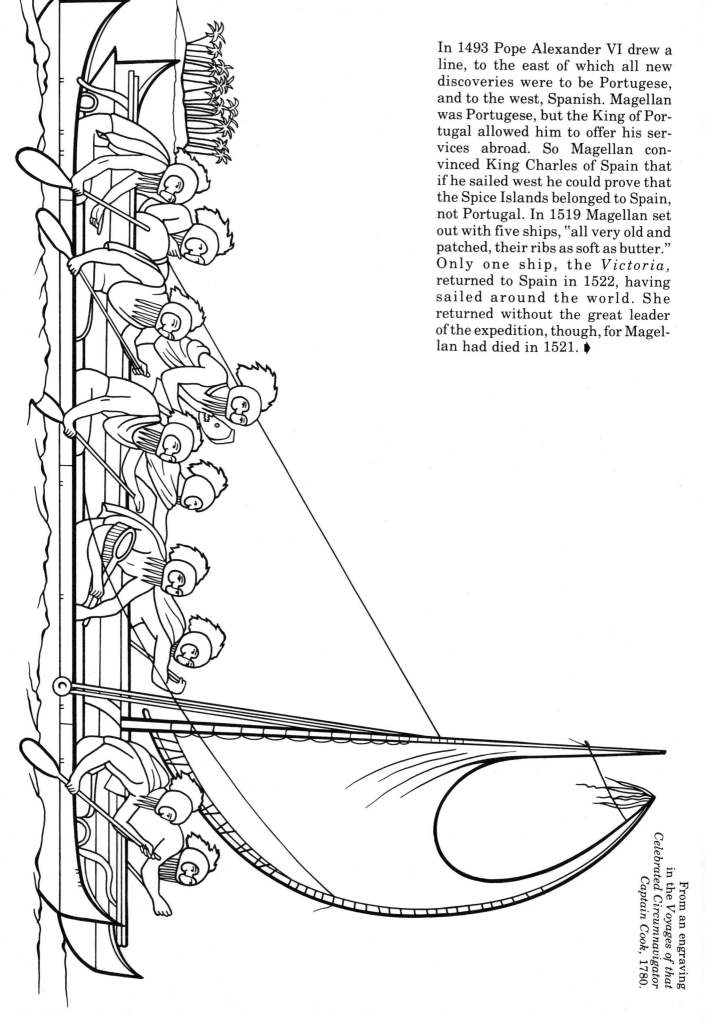

In 1493 Pope Alexander VI drew a line, to the east of which all new discoveries were to be Portugese, and to the west, Spanish. Magellan was Portugese, but the King of Portugal allowed him to offer his services abroad. So Magellan convinced King Charles of Spain that if he sailed west he could prove that the Spice Islands belonged to Spain, not Portugal. In 1519 Magellan set out with five ships, "all very old and patched, their ribs as soft as butter." Only one ship, the *Victoria,* returned to Spain in 1522, having sailed around the world. She returned without the great leader of the expedition, though, for Magellan had died in 1521. ◗

The Pacific Ocean was explored centuries before Magellan by such hardy sailors as these masked Hawaiians.

From an engraving in the *Voyages of that Celebrated Circumnavigator Captain Cook,* 1780.

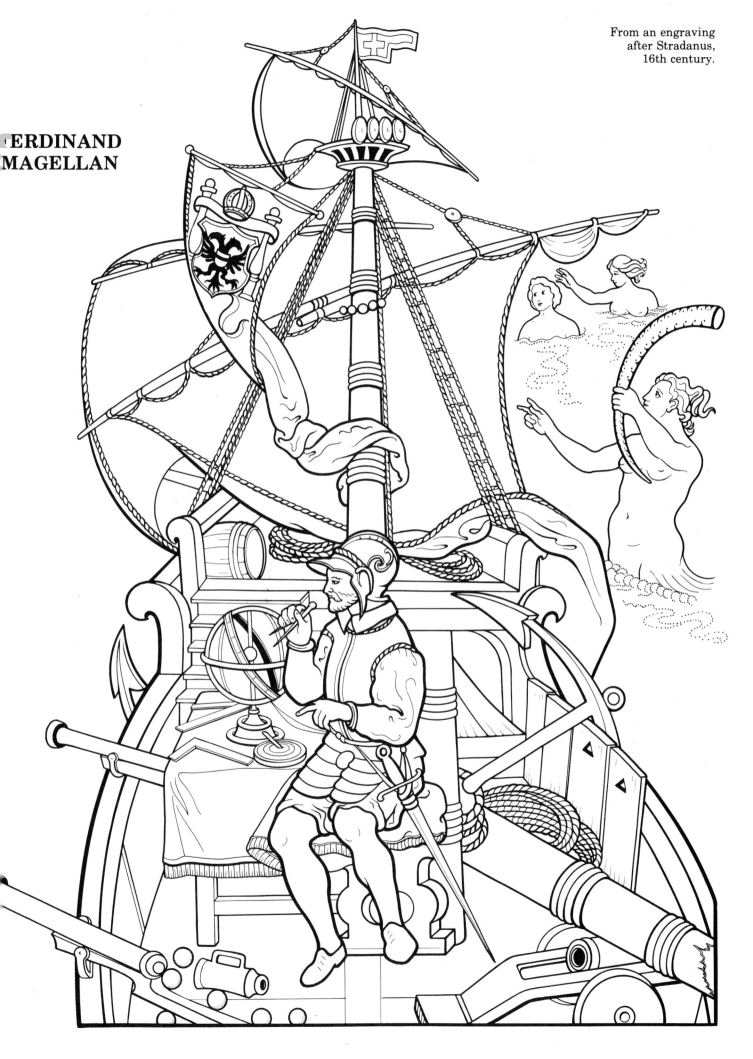

FERDINAND
MAGELLAN

From an engraving
after Stradanus,
16th century.

THE GOLDEN HIND
CAPTURING A RICH SPANISH SHIP

Sir Francis Drake left Plymouth on his famous voyage around the world on December 13, 1577. His own ship was the *Pelican,* which was later renamed the *Golden Hind* in honor of Sir Christopher Hatton — one of the exploration's investors and an important person at Queen Elizabeth I's court. Drake had four other ships with him: the *Elizabeth,* the *Marigold,* the *Swan,* and the *Benedict.* Drake sailed first to the Cape Verde Islands, where he captured an experienced Portugese pilot, and then on to the coast of South America, to Port St. Julian, where Magellan had been 58 years before. On August 20, 1578, the passage through the Strait of Magellan was begun, and 16 days later the Pacific Ocean was reached — and terrible storms. Three ships were now lost, and the *Elizabeth* sailed back through the strait to England. The *Golden Hind* was alone in waters which had belonged to Spain for many years. Drake sailed up the coast of Chile and into the harbor of Valparaiso, where he captured gold and supplies. On February 15, 1579 he reached Callao, the harbor of Lima, capital of Peru. Here he heard of a rich Spanish treasure ship which had left 12 days earlier for Panama. In the scene above, the *Golden Hind* is capturing this rich ship, the *Neustra Señora de la Concepción.* Drake then sailed up the coast of California and spent several weeks in June and July, 1579, near San Francisco Bay. On July 23rd the *Golden Hind* set out across the Pacific Ocean, and by way of the Philippines, Java, the Indian Ocean and the Cape of Good Hope, was back in Plymouth on September 26, 1580, with enough treasure to pay off the Queen's foreign debts and to found new trading companies.

On August 10, 1628 a beautiful new warship was launched in Stockholm Harbor. Suddenly a squall caused her to heel over and take in water through her open gun ports. The WASA, built by a Dutch shipwright for the great young Swedish King Gustavus Adolphus (a hero of the Thirty Years War), sank in 110 feet of water, where she lay for 333 years. Neither worms nor storms had destroyed the ship, which has been spectacularly raised and can be seen when you visit Stockholm.

From drawings in the National Maritime Museum, Greenwich.

THE VAN DE VELDES' YACHT, 1675

Ships reached their greatest beauty during the 17th century, for gloriously gilded carvings replaced the simpler painted patterns of the 16th century. This was also the golden age of sea painting, and among the greatest marine artists were the Van de Veldes, Willem the Elder (1611-1693) and Willem the Younger (1633-1707). This is a yacht which they designed for themselves, from which they made their sketches of the great ships and battles. They worked in both Holland and England, and many museums now have some of their paintings and accurate drawings.

From an engraving after
Willem Van de Velde
the Elder, 1639.

THE AMELIA,
FLAGSHIP OF THE
INDOMITABLE DUTCH
ADMIRAL MARTIN
HARPERTSZ TROMP

AMELIA

The Dutch Wars were fought
over commerce. The English
won because they had superior
ships, but they had no sailors
superior to Martin Tromp. His
loss in the battle of 1653 off the
Texel "caused grass to grow in
the streets of Amsterdam."

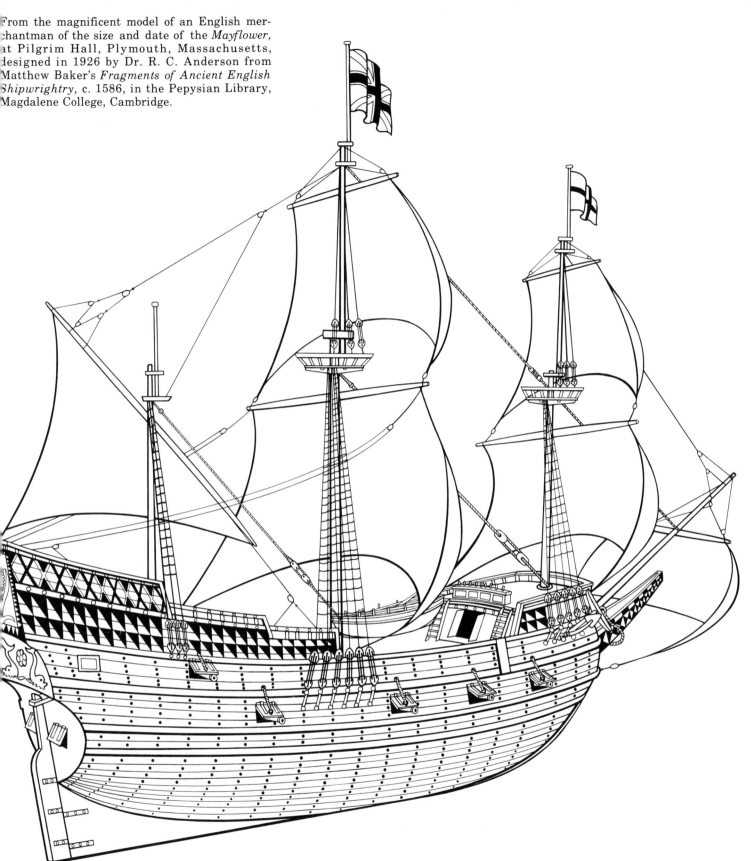

THE MAYFLOWER

The *Mayflower* was an old ship when she sailed
for America in 1620, and she may have been
the *Mayflower* that served in 1588 in the
Armada fighting. She had been employed in
trading voyages to La Rochelle and Bordeaux,
and occasionally to Norway and Hamburg. She
was probably about 90 feet in length from stem
to sternpost. The *Mayflower* was described by
Robert Cushman, one of the organizers of the
trip in 1620, as a fine ship, but Captain John
Smith called her a "leaking unwholesome ship."
The Atlantic crossing took an arduous 66 days.

THE WASA

From a woodcut by
Cesare Vecellio, 1571

A VENETIAN GALLEY RETURNING HOME AFTER THE VICTORY AT LEPANTO, 1571

At the battle of Lepanto the fleets of Venice, Spain and the Pope finally defeated the Turks. Each side had more than 200 large galleys and sailing galleasses, and the Turks lost most of theirs. Here the Venetians announce the news with cannon and drums, as they bring home the captured flags. But the Sultan said that the loss of his fleet was only like the loss of a beard, and he immediately grew another gigantic navy.

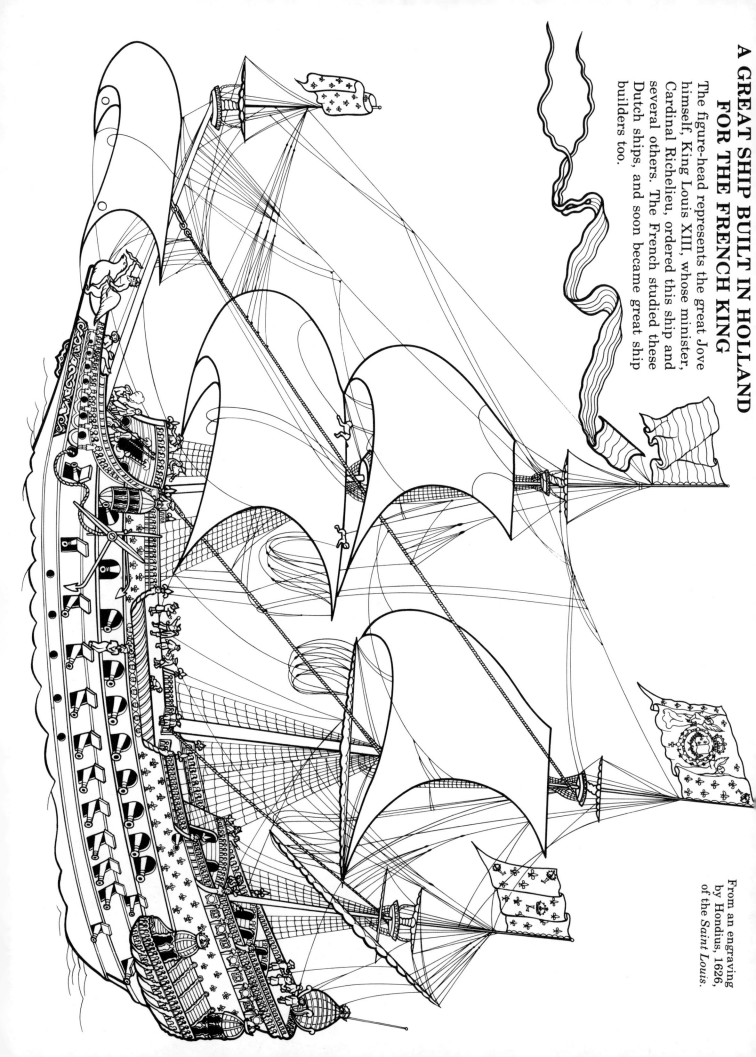

A GREAT SHIP BUILT IN HOLLAND FOR THE FRENCH KING

The figure-head represents the great Jove himself, King Louis XIII, whose minister, Cardinal Richelieu, ordered this ship and several others. The French studied these Dutch ships, and soon became great ship builders too.

From an engraving
by Hondius, 1626,
of the *Saint Louis*.

From an engraving by Breughel, 1565.

A MAN-OF-WAR
FROM DRAKE'S TIME

This ship should be colored very brightly, for that is how ships were painted during the time of Queen Elizabeth I. But ships also began to be really seaworthy. Drake, in his voyage around the world in 1577-1580, went from Java to Sierra Leone, 8500 miles, without touching a single port.

The **ARK ROYAL** was Lord Howard of Effingham's flagship against the Invincible Armada.

THE MEDITERRANEAN XEBEC

This vessel, with three lateen sails, is a sailing descendant of the medieval galley. It was a favorite ship of the Barbary pirates, and was also used by the Spanish navy until 1827. A similar craft is the Arab *dhow*, which is still in use in the Red and Arabian Seas.

From a painting of the schooner Baltic, built in 1763 at Newbury, Massachusetts; Peabody Museum, Salem.

THE SCHOONER BALTIC

This is the type of ship in which New England privateersmen put to sea during the American Revolution. Paintings of American ships as old as this are very rare. Such little ships as this captured 800 British ships, all carrying badly needed supplies.

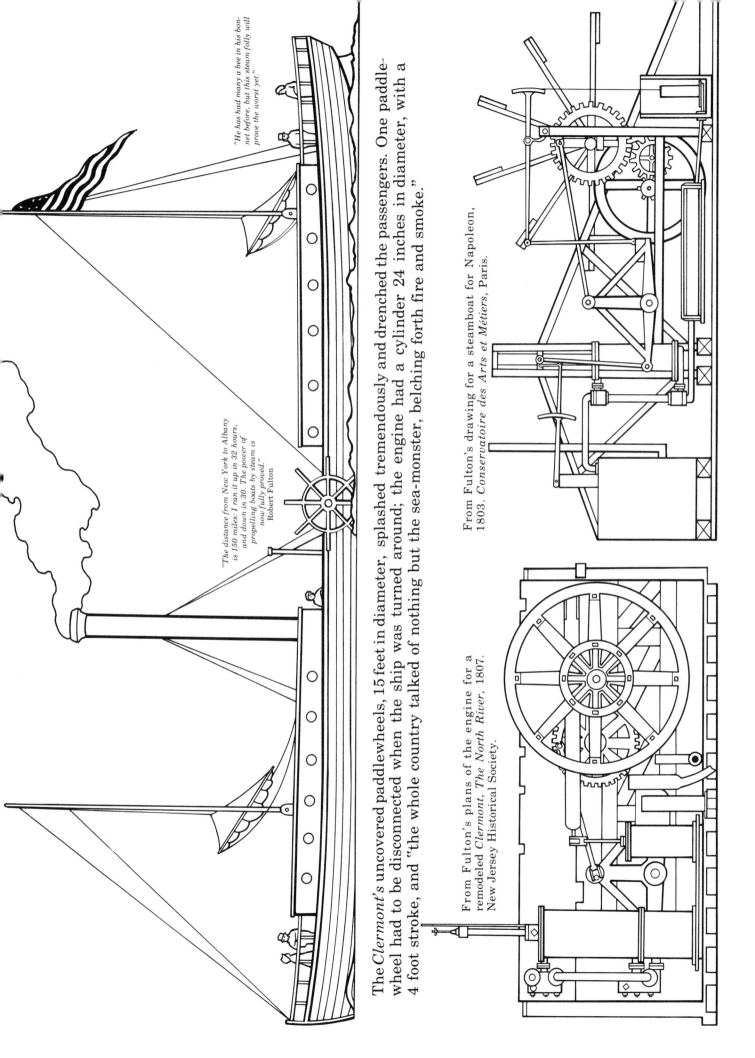

"He has had many a bee in his bonnet before, but this steam folly will prove the worst yet."

"The distance from New York to Albany is 150 miles: I ran it up in 32 hours, and down in 30. The power of propelling boats by steam is now fully proved."
Robert Fulton

The *Clermont's* uncovered paddlewheels, 15 feet in diameter, splashed tremendously and drenched the passengers. One paddle-wheel had to be disconnected when the ship was turned around; the engine had a cylinder 24 inches in diameter, with a 4 foot stroke, and "the whole country talked of nothing but the sea-monster, belching forth fire and smoke."

From Fulton's drawing for a steamboat for Napoleon, 1803. *Conservatoire des Arts et Métiers,* Paris.

From Fulton's plans of the engine for a remodeled *Clermont, The North River,* 1807. New Jersey Historical Society.

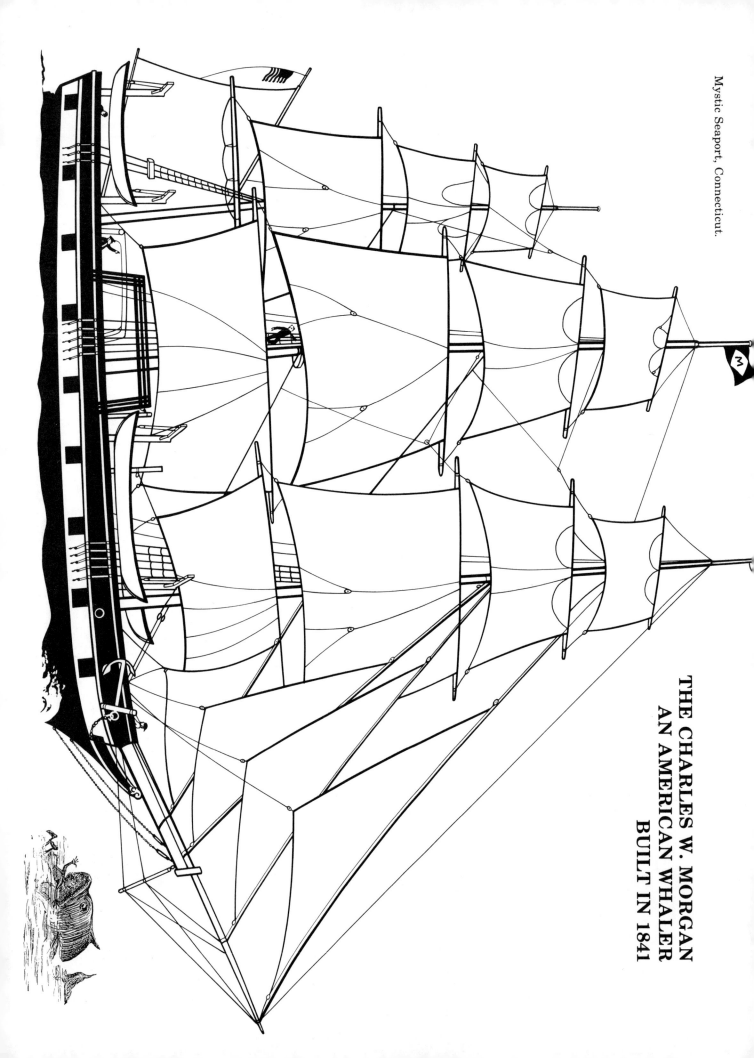

Mystic Seaport, Connecticut.

THE CHARLES W. MORGAN
AN AMERICAN WHALER
BUILT IN 1841

From a drawing attributed to J.W. Orr, of Buffalo; 1837, Peabody Museum, Salem, Mass.

A GREAT LAKES STEAMER

CONSTELLATION.

Fulton and his partner Livingston were given a steamboat monopoly by New York, but this was knocked down by the Supreme Court in 1824. There had been few steamers on the Great Lakes before, mostly Canadian, but now steamboating was free for all. The Erie Canal opened in 1825 and connected the Great Lakes to the Atlantic Ocean. From Buffalo at the end of the canal went settlers to the harbors of Chicago, St. Joseph and Green Bay. The Chicago Line (2 ships) was started in 1838 with the *Constellation* and the *Pennsylvania* making sailings from Buffalo to Chicago every two weeks. The large forests along the shores provided wood for fuel, and the ships made 12 miles per hour. A round trip took about 20 days.

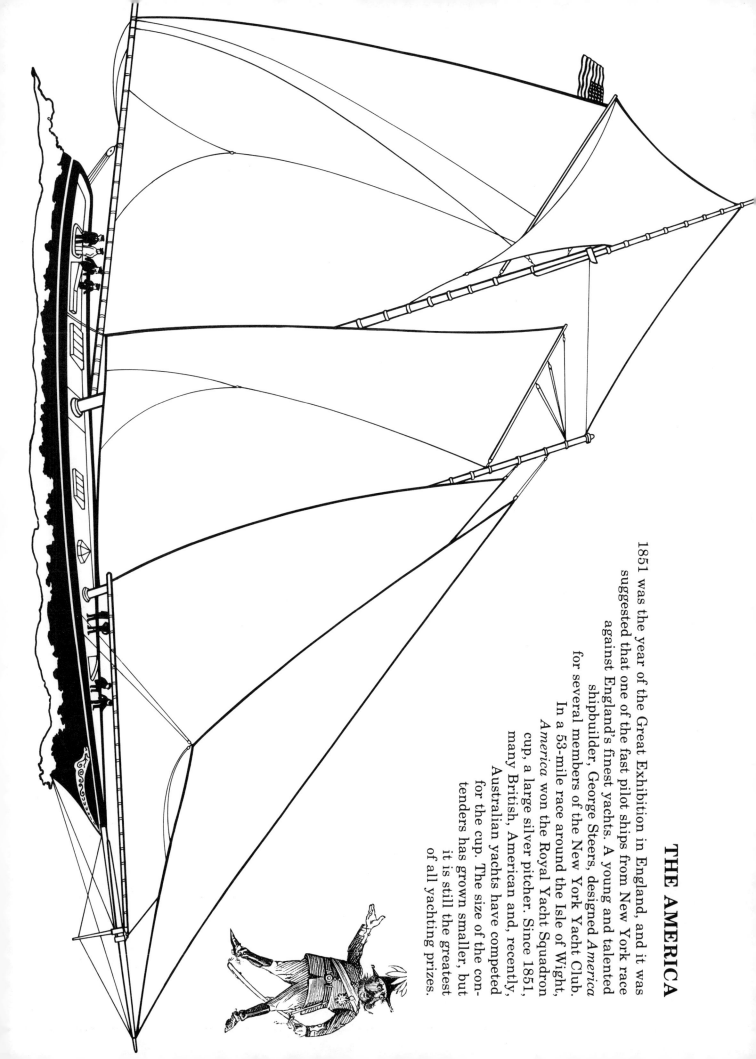

THE AMERICA

1851 was the year of the Great Exhibition in England, and it was suggested that one of the fast pilot ships from New York race against England's finest yachts. A young and talented shipbuilder, George Steers, designed *America* for several members of the New York Yacht Club. In a 53-mile race around the Isle of Wight, *America* won the Royal Yacht Squadron cup, a large silver pitcher. Since 1851, many British, American and, recently, Australian yachts have competed for the cup. The size of the contenders has grown smaller, but it is still the greatest of all yachting prizes.

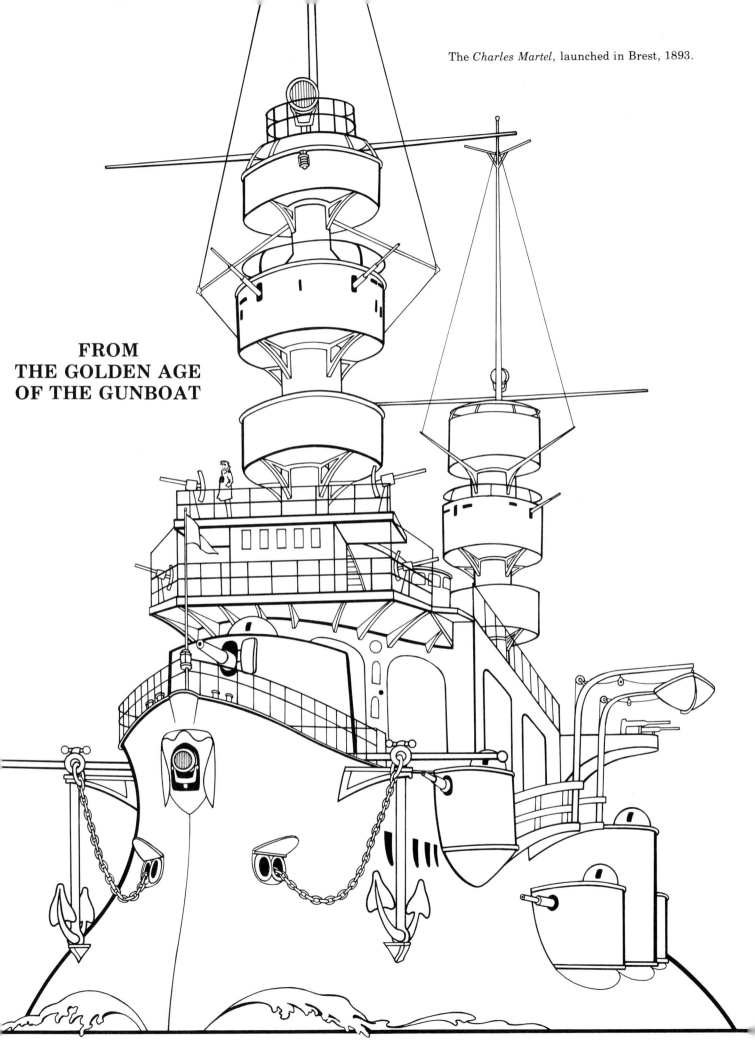

The *Charles Martel*, launched in Brest, 1893.

**FROM
THE GOLDEN AGE
OF THE GUNBOAT**

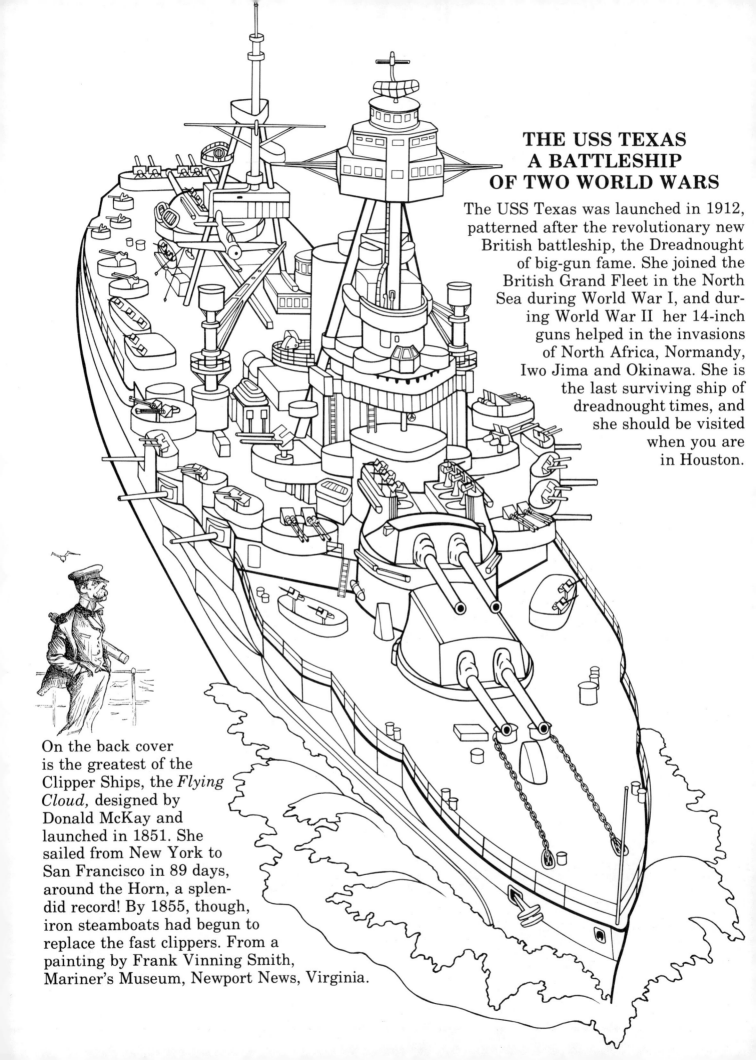

THE USS TEXAS
A BATTLESHIP
OF TWO WORLD WARS

The USS Texas was launched in 1912,
patterned after the revolutionary new
British battleship, the Dreadnought
of big-gun fame. She joined the
British Grand Fleet in the North
Sea during World War I, and during World War II her 14-inch
guns helped in the invasions
of North Africa, Normandy,
Iwo Jima and Okinawa. She is
the last surviving ship of
dreadnought times, and
she should be visited
when you are
in Houston.

On the back cover
is the greatest of the
Clipper Ships, the *Flying
Cloud,* designed by
Donald McKay and
launched in 1851. She
sailed from New York to
San Francisco in 89 days,
around the Horn, a splen-
did record! By 1855, though,
iron steamboats had begun to
replace the fast clippers. From a
painting by Frank Vinning Smith,
Mariner's Museum, Newport News, Virginia.